美国

How We Organize Ourselves | Non-Fiction Series

Copyright © 2022 by Level Learning, INC. and Washington Yu Ying PCS™
Original and Edited Text Copyright © 2022 by Washington Yu Ying PCS™

All rights reserved. No part of this book in whole or part may be reproduced without written permission from the publisher.

Published by Level Learning, INC.

Content Contributors:
Washington Yu Ying PCS™ - Qianyi (Shirley) Zhang, Pearl Zao He You
Level Learning - Jingyao Qi

Illustrations by: Josh Taira

Leveling classification based on Level Learning standard.
For full description, visit www.levellearning.com

ISBN 978-1-64040-111-2
Simplified Chinese Edition

About Level Learning:

Level Learning provides a literacy focused curriculum specifically designed for K-12 Chinese as a Second Language classrooms. Our program offers 20 levels of specific and detailed objectives, leveled texts and passages, mastery-based online assessment, and analytics to enable data-driven instruction. Level Learning reading curriculum for both literature and informational text emphasize grammar and comprehension skills to help teachers develop confident and independent Chinese language readers. The non-fiction series of books are specifically designed to support our informational text course based on multiple national standards. To learn more about our entire offering, visit www.levellearning.com.

About Washington Yu Ying PCS™:

Washington Yu Ying PCS is a Mandarin English dual language immersion International Baccalaureate (IB) World school. Yu Ying's mission is to inspire and prepare young people to create a better world by challenging them to reach their full potential in a nurturing Chinese/English educational environment. Yu Ying's comprehensive IB, dual immersion curriculum equips students with global competencies for success in the real world. As a leader in immersion education, Yu Ying is determined to advance Chinese language programs and global citizenry education by helping other schools create and strengthen their Chinese programs. For more information, email: products@washingtonyuying.org

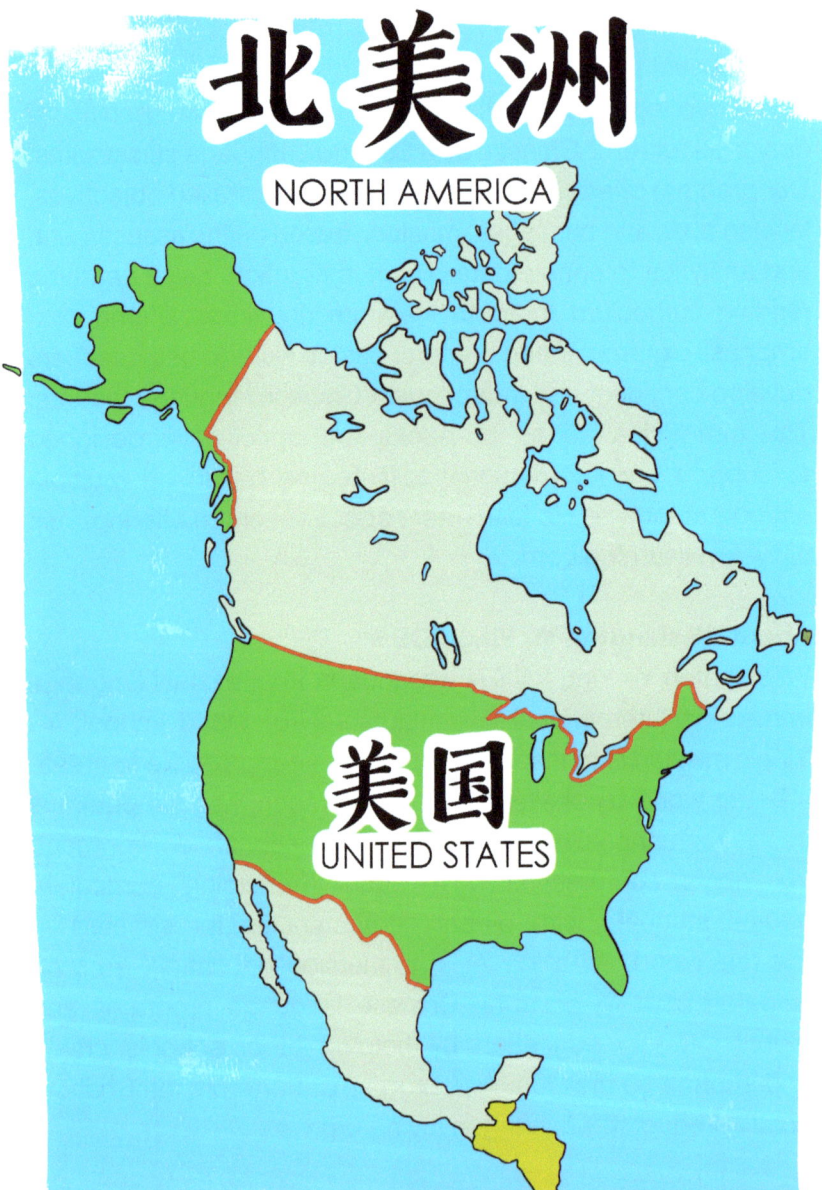

美国是一个美丽的国家。

美国在北美洲。

美国的北边是加拿大。

美国的南边是墨西哥。

美国的东边是大西洋。

美国的西边是太平洋。

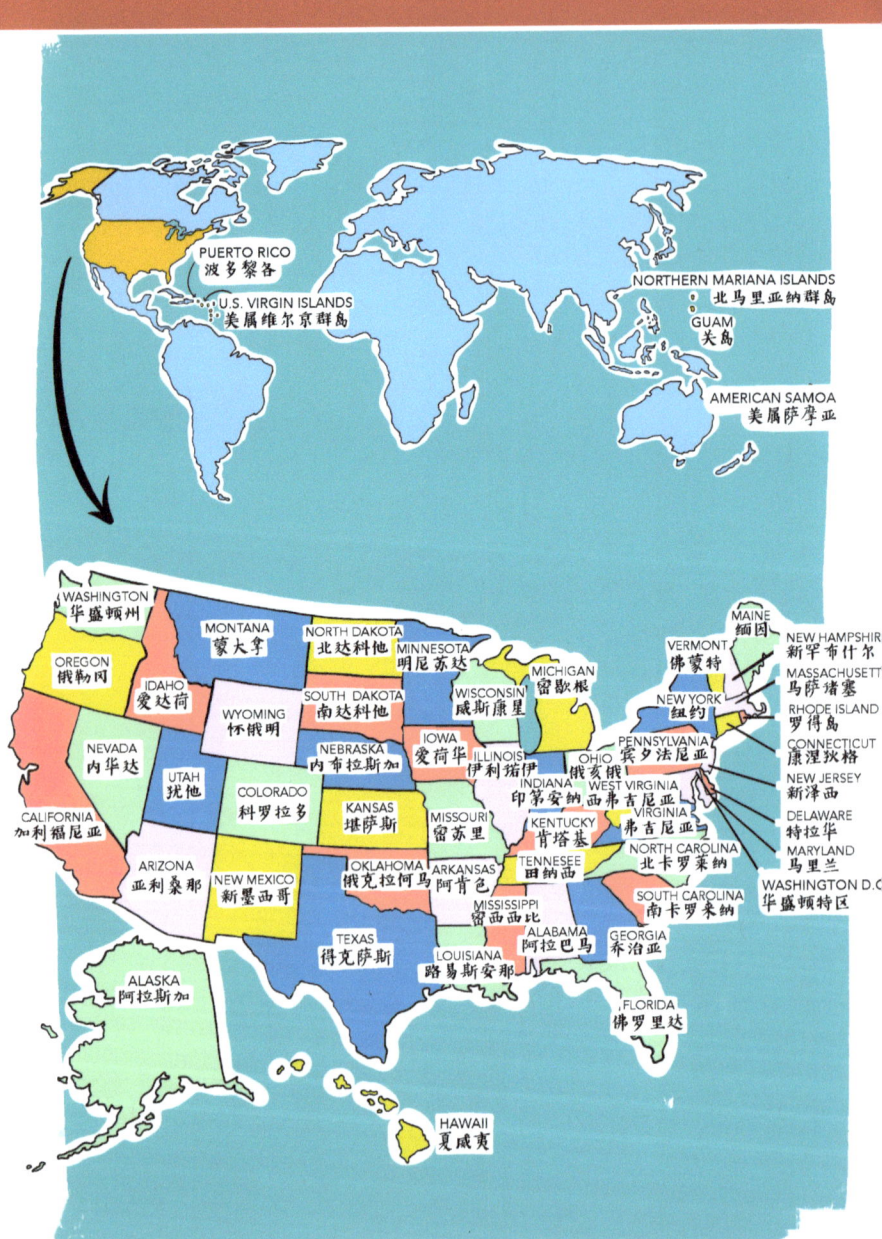

美国有50个州。

美国还有一个特区和五个属地。

美国有许多国家公园。

这些公园都很美丽。

美国有许多野生动物。

这些动物都很珍贵。

在美国，很多人来自不同的国家。

他们说不同的语言。

Glossary

	Pinyin	English Definition
美国	měi guó	U.S.A.
美丽	měi lì	beautiful
国家	guó jiā	country
北美洲	běi měi zhōu	North America
北	běi	north
边	biān	side
加拿大	jiā ná dà	Canada
南	nán	south
墨西哥	mò xī gē	Mexico
东	dōng	east
大西洋	dà xī yáng	Atlantic Ocean
西	xī	west
太平洋	tài píng yáng	Pacific Ocean
州	zhōu	state
特区	tè qū	district

	Pinyin	English Definition
属地	shǔ dì	territory
许多	xǔ duō	many
国家公园	guó jiā gōng yuán	National Park
很	hěn	very
野生动物	yě shēng dòng wù	wild animal
珍贵	zhēn guì	precious
不同	bù tóng	different
语言	yǔ yán	language

www.ingramcontent.com/pod-product-compliance
Lightning Source LLC
Chambersburg PA
CBHW041226070526
44584CB00001B/114